RENOVATING TRADITIONAL BUILDINGS

AN OWNER'S GUIDE

Author

Calum Maclean RIAS RIBA

First Edition

July 2015

AIDH : NORTH
ARCHITECTURE & INTERIOR DESIGN HUB

info@aidh.co.uk
www.aidh.co.uk

Acknowledgements

I would like to take this opportunity to thank everyone that
offered their support, comments and feedback in the production of this book.

A special mention goes to
John Duncan FRIAS IHBC

First published in the United Kingdom in 2015 by The Choir Press

ISBN 978-1-910864-24-1

About the Author

*Calum Maclean is a director of the Inverness architectural practice, **AIDH:NORTH** and is an RIAS accredited conservation architect.*

He is a member of the Royal Incorporation of Architects in Scotland and has over 20 years' experience working with private and public sector clients in both Scotland and the Republic of Ireland.

Calum grew up in Caithness in the North of Scotland before studying Architecture at Edinburgh College of Art.

Throughout his life he has worked in towns and countryside that enjoy some of the finest examples of traditional buildings which have survived centuries of change. These buildings provide a richness and beauty to the culture and identity of each community.

This appreciation has ultimately inspired his guiding principle that architecture, whether traditional or contemporary, tells us the story of people's lives. We should take care to ensure the story is told well and shared with others.

CONTENTS

WELCOME

Many people struggle with the challenges of renovating, modifying and maintaining traditional buildings.

Traditional buildings are resilient structures that have often lasted for hundreds of years. Beautifully crafted from high-quality materials, they sit well in a landscape that has matured around them. There is no reason why these buildings cannot be updated and adapted to provide beautiful, practical accommodation long into the future, but they can present some new and unique challenges to anyone who is unfamiliar with them.

The good news is that there are many craftsmen specialising in traditional building methods. The bad news is that within the regular, everyday construction community much of the knowledge and skill required for working with traditional buildings and materials has been lost.

It is not surprising that owners of traditional buildings often find it hard to get good advice and it often comes too late to avoid costly mistakes.

Don't despair; this book is going to help you achieve your goals, steer you around common problems and save you a lot of heartache. Careful planning and a methodical approach are the keys to a successful project. This book is written in a concise and simple format to get these core messages across quickly and effectively.

This is not a technical manual.

If you are looking for a book that focuses on detailed technical advice regarding the practical application of conservation techniques, this is not the book for you. Or maybe it is ... you just don't realise it yet.

I hope that you enjoy this guide

CHAPTER ONE :

INTRODUCTION

Traditional buildings tend to be over 100 years old and were built before cars and lorries were commonplace. Since it wasn't possible to transport materials very far, buildings were constructed from natural materials like stone, timber and slate that were found close to where they were built.

Built with solid, thick walls and steeply pitched roofs, these buildings tended to have a simple layout that responded to local climate and ground conditions. Using local knowledge, the builders were able to maximise building performance and to minimise the use of scarce or costly materials.

Natural variations in the geology and climate give the building materials a unique colouring and texture that binds them to their location. This is not only important to their appearance but also contributes to the unique character and identity associated with communities that built them.

Traditional buildings offer a valuable insight to the history and lifestyles of ordinary people and illustrate the changing fortunes of each community across the generations.

Just as they were important to the people who built them all those years ago, they are a valuable resource to us today. The re-use of traditional buildings is an important part of a sustainable strategy that promotes environmental protection and tackles climate change.

We are fortunate to have many, many traditional buildings in our countryside and towns. Many are used as private homes, some are used for community activities and some are empty or abandoned.

Sadly too many are suffering from a lack of care and attention but that can all change and this book will hopefully encourage you to appreciate the value of your building and help you to look after it properly.

The starting point for each renovation or maintenance project is unique. It may be an opportunity to create a home or office that has a unique and distinctive character and identity. It may be as a result of supporting your local community and volunteering to improve the condition of a building that provides an important space for social activities.

Whatever the reason, the prospect of starting the build and the anticipation of moving in to your newly refurbished property will spur you on. However, it is important to approach the project in the right way. The enthusiasm and passion you bring to the project must be accompanied by an approach that embraces the history of the building and promotes a spirit of enquiry to ensure that the proposals work in harmony with the existing structure.

In the following pages you will find valuable insights and advice that will help you to avoid costly and frustrating mistakes. You will gain an understanding of the task ahead: how to plan the development in a logical way, where to find people who can offer reliable knowledge and advice, how to budget for the work, how long the process will take and, most importantly, the key steps you need to take to ensure that your project is a success.

Working with a traditional building is not just about checking off tasks on a list and organising tradesmen; it should also be an enjoyable and rewarding experience. So before we delve into the planning stage, it is important to spend some time thinking about what the project will mean to you.

To get you started, I have split this chapter into three segments called 'The Three "C"s'.

All traditional buildings, however modest and seemingly abandoned or forgotten, share the qualities discussed in each segment. Once you have discovered these qualities in your own building, you will have a better understanding of the process that will follow.

There is a wealth of architecture and design philosophy that has laid the foundations for this approach and I would encourage anyone with an interest to explore it further, but that is not the purpose of this book. Today I will only touch lightly on these ideas, in order to introduce you to a way of thinking that will help you to uncover the true nature of the project, to frame your requirements in an intelligent way and to identify the means to achieve them.

THE THREE 'C'S

CONTEXT

Modern buildings are generally constructed from mass-produced materials that are manufactured hundreds of miles away, often in foreign countries. These materials are distributed around the world to be assembled on any site, seemingly at random.

Modern construction materials reflect the current trends in technology that encourage a throwaway culture. Composite products are manufactured with complex components, built to a budget, designed with a limited lifespan to be used and discarded when no longer required.

In contrast to their modern counterparts, traditional buildings have a very close relationship with their surroundings. The colour and texture of the materials reflect the local geology. The layout of the buildings in the landscape responds to climate, reflects historic patterns of land use and reveals important links between communities.

We need to pause for reflection, change our thinking and adopt a longer-term view.

These buildings use high quality durable materials that can be readily maintained and adapted to suit changing needs. They can have a life of hundreds of years. Our involvement will be a fleeting one and part of a much bigger story.

Whether as part of a mature landscape or an urban streetscape, traditional buildings form part of a wider composition that is integral to our understanding of place and identity. They become the backdrop to many events and memories that shape our communities, and they deserve to be treated with care and respect.

The value of these buildings to the community is often recognised publicly. Local authorities maintain a list of buildings of special architectural or cultural significance. These are afforded protection through planning policy and enforcement. Your building may also be **listed**. It is important to check before you do anything as it is an offence to make alterations to a listed building without the appropriate permission.

The statutory protection of historic buildings is important, but regulation is no substitute for a proper understanding of these buildings.

If you find yourself frustrated by regulations that seem to be getting in the way of your plans, take a step back for a moment. More often than not you are approaching the task in the wrong way.

CHARACTER

Traditional buildings have bags of character.

Their age confers a dignity and beauty which sets them apart from modern building. It's a quality that can be admired but never re-created.

The older the building, the more often it will have been adapted to changing needs, circumstances, fashion and tastes. The accumulation of memories from previous generations gives traditional buildings their unique character and identity; sometimes quirky, sometimes mysterious.

While the building and its setting will tell us about the community, when you look up close you will find the marks and imprints of the individuals who have been a part of the building's history.

Try to uncover the features, marks and blemishes that give your building its unique feel. They will reveal the story of your building and its relationship with its surroundings. Don't forget to record your discoveries and share them with others.

COLLABORATION

Being part of a bigger story also means that we need to add our own chapter which others can follow.

You need not be limited in your aspirations for the property. There are many approaches that can be taken offering a broad range of design styles and outcomes, from conservation and restorations where buildings are faithfully preserved, to contemporary interventions which combine and contrast with the historic structure.

One note of caution. Be careful when mixing styles. It requires a lot of talent, attention to detail and a comprehensive understanding of the design theory and history that underpins both genres, if it is going to create a meaningful and intelligent dialogue between old and new.

Working with the fabric of the building means not only retaining the visual appearance; it also means retaining the essential backbone of the structure and the underlying architecture of the spaces. If you can embrace this approach, you will have a robust building that will continue to perform well and be a valuable asset, indefinitely.

A drastic intervention that cuts across this fabric to suit your immediate needs may work for now, but later on it will compromise the ability of the building to adapt to new uses in the future. You will create problems that are difficult and costly to resolve. Not being able to adapt to changing needs in the future may lead to a lack of investment and a gradual decline in the building's fortunes in the years ahead. This a poor outcome for the building's and it is also a poor outcome for communities, businesses and home owners as they are left struggling to find suitable spaces for their activities.

Traditional buildings are very resilient, more so than their modern counterparts. A careful, systematic approach to renovation and maintenance will transform these buildings into attractive, healthy, sustainable and practical buildings ideally suited to any purpose.

If you work imaginatively with the original structure rather than seeing it as an obstruction to development, attractive spaces can be created to generate a 'wow factor' that is both unique and memorable.

Chapter Two :

7 Traps to Be Avoided

Are you ready ?

You may now be picturing yourself in your newly renovated building, where everything has turned out exactly as you planned it. Your efforts have transformed the property and, in turn, have improved your use and enjoyment of the space beyond your wildest expectations.

Hold on to that vision and nurture it carefully. I am about to bring you back down to earth. I am going to ask you to pause and take a deep breath as I lead you around some of the many traps that are waiting to ensnare you and sap every ounce of your energy.

A cold shower is rarely an enticing prospect, but sharpened wits will be alert to potential problems, which is a necessary first step in the adoption of an approach that will help you to avoid them.

Don't worry, if you make it through this stage, there is a reward waiting for you. I will give you some useful strategies that will restore your enthusiasm.

Trap Number 1
FORGETTING WHY YOU STARTED

It is easy to get bogged down by the complexity of the process and forget about the vision that inspired you in the first place: the dream of attractive spaces set in beautiful surroundings that would allow you to carry out your daily routine effortlessly.

These aspirations should remain the focus of everything that is done throughout the development of the project. Don't let them get overwhelmed by the technicalities of the project.

The quality of the spaces we inhabit has a major impact on our emotional well-being. Whether for a home or an office, well-designed spaces will bring a sense of pride and satisfaction whereas a poor environment will be a constant source of frustration, intruding on our thoughts and activities.

It is important to spend time thinking about the look and feel that you wish to create once the work is complete. Consider not only the size and the sequence of spaces but also the colour, texture and light. You should consider activities that are going to take place and the style of furnishings you will use, as these will all combine to create an identity that reflects your values and aspirations.

This requires a reflection on our personal and emotional responses to the spaces we inhabit, which some may find difficult to discuss.

Don't be shy. It is important that you share these ideas with your architect. Your architect will help you to filter and refine these ideas, combining them into a structured and intelligent strategy that will inform the rest of the process.

You may think that the artistic and emotive characteristics of design are more relevant to the home environment, but every successful businessman understands the important influence of design on brand identity and its role in communicating a company's values to its customers.

The best designs will create the feel you want whilst also embracing the character of the existing building.

Unlike a new build, you are not starting with a blank page. You are building a relationship with the existing building.

If you were involved in the initial acquisition of the property, there will have been features and characteristics over and above price and location that clinched the deal. Focus on retaining these characteristics and make them the starting point for any future proposals.

The existing building will create a framework that will support your design aspirations. It is important that you understand it. Pay attention to the details, study the proportion of spaces and openings. Learn how these influence the feeling of the internal and external spaces and use these as a template or starting point.

As mentioned in the introduction, with your design you are creating a new chapter to an existing story. This need not restrict your creativity or imagination. There are a wide range of themes and styles that can be explored, from the period to the contemporary, whilst still maintaining a meaningful dialogue and continuity with the historic building fabric.

Trap Number 2

FALSE ECONOMIES

There are many projects that are constrained by cost and however hard you try, the budget just will not stretch to deliver everything that you hoped for.

It can be tempting to try and economise on one area of the project in order to gain a little bit more, somewhere else. At moments like these you may think professional advice is a luxury, whereas expenditure on contractors and suppliers will at least result in the delivery of a tangible product: something you can see and touch.

When the scope of the work is small, as in minor repairs or maintenance, your first thoughts may be to approach a tradesman directly. There are two problems with this:

1. Most tradesmen these days work almost exclusively with modern materials. When alterations or repairs are made to traditional buildings using modern construction techniques and modern materials, problems can be compounded, causing more damage and a great deal of frustration.

2. Attempting to isolate smaller manageable packages of work can often prove difficult. Many aspects of a building's structure and its internal environment are interrelated and cannot be addressed in isolation; a change in one area will have consequences in another. Before you know it, a small job has quickly grown into a tangled mess.

A less scrupulous tradesman will start work and then uncover one problem after another, expecting you to keep paying with no end to the work in sight. A responsible tradesman knows that a systematic approach that considers the potential wider consequences for the building as a whole is essential.

This means that a responsible tradesman will immediately refer you to a professional to carry out investigations and prepare a detailed schedule of works, so that it is clear what the tradesman has to price for and what your expectations are.

Older buildings may appear to have a simple method of construction. They are in fact highly sophisticated. The use of materials and construction techniques evolved over many hundreds of years to create buildings that are highly attuned and responsive to their surroundings.

Trying to save costs on professional advice is rarely successful. When we all lead busy lives, few of us have the time or energy to carry out the research required to deliver a successful construction project. At times when the budget demands difficult decisions, it is more important than ever to have someone by your side who will help you choose wisely.

Conservation architects are trained not just to make a project pretty, but to match the right building methods and the right materials to the needs of your building. They have a broad range of skills and expertise built up over many years of working with these buildings.

Your conservation architect will be able to guide you through the process, review budgets, discuss alternative options, anticipate issues that need to be addressed in advance and help you select tradesmen with the right skills to carry out the work needed.

With help to prepare and plan the project in advance, many costly and time-consuming mistakes will be avoided. Not only that, you will benefit from improved quality in the finished project.

Sometimes lifting a floorboard or opening a wall uncovers an example of previous attempts to modernise the property.

Here, the installation of electrical or plumbing services has been undertaken without any understanding of the historic building fabric and has resulted in significant structural damage to the timber floor that needed to be repaired at great cost.

A small maintenance task, repointing of stonework, has resulted in significant and costly damage.

Modern materials like cement are incompatible with traditional materials like natural stone, causing deterioration and erosion. Neither client nor builder knew any better.

A couple of hours with a conservation architect would have saved the client thousands of pounds in repair work.

Trap Number 3
RUSHING TO ACTION

'Marry in haste, repent at leisure.'

The more information that you can gather about the building before work starts, the more likely you are to avoid a nasty surprise.

Traditional and historic buildings require special care. The amount and type of investigation required will vary depending on the particular characteristics of your property. Your architect will be able to give advice on the most appropriate and effective way to proceed.

The internal structure is invariably hidden from view by wall and ceiling linings. Naturally, you will want as few unsightly holes knocked in plaster finishes as possible. Experience and expertise are required to obtain the best results with the least disruption.

Bear in mind that however diligent the investigatory work is, some assumptions will still have to be made about the underlying structure; there will be no certainty until work starts and the walls are opened up.

A rush to action can lead to a simplistic solution that treats the symptom rather than the cause. Traditional materials have a sophisticated internal structure. The results of any investigation need to be interpreted carefully and may result in a diagnosis and a solution that may not have been obvious.

Modern materials tend to be hard, inflexible and impervious to water vapour, meaning that they don't breathe. Traditional materials, on the other hand are soft, flexible and breathable. These two types of materials will react differently to changing internal and external temperature and humidity.

These compatibility issues need to be considered carefully when planning new works. It is important that materials and techniques are chosen that will work together and in harmony with the historic structure.

Be particularly careful when considering chemical treatments. It is likely that you will encounter companies that will promote solutions that are accompanied by guarantees and assurance. They often mask a problem rather than solving it. Unlike timber and masonry interventions, these will be irreversible and can do lasting damage.

Even when working with traditional materials, expertise is important. For example, there are many varieties of sandstone. Sandstone from two different quarries may appear the same but will have very different microscopic structures and properties. Laid incorrectly or used together in the wrong situation, these two types of stone will react differently to their environment, causing damage.

Further issues can arise when building services, such as heating, plumbing, electrics or telecoms installations, are installed or upgraded. Installers often overlook the impact that their work will have on historic building fabric and they can cause a great deal of damage.

In addition to the technical issues, traditional properties can often become home to protected wildlife and bats can sometimes roost in concealed spaces. These will not necessarily prevent work taking place, but there are strict legal procedures that must be followed when dealing with these situations.

Trap Number 4

PUTTING THE CART BEFORE THE HORSE

Don't invest substantial sums on cosmetic issues when there are underlying structural issues that need to be sorted first. This seems like common sense, but it is easy to get thrown off balance when offers of financial assistance appear too good to miss.

Governments often develop incentives to achieve their policy objectives. The drive to reduce carbon emissions has seen the emergence of numerous schemes designed to encourage property owners to improve the energy performance of their building fabric, either through insulation or by updating heating systems and incorporating microgeneration technology.

With the opportunity to secure substantial sums of money towards the cost of these improvements, it is hardly surprising that these schemes attract a lot of attention. The situation can be exaggerated further by the short-term view that governments tend to take in these matters. The window of opportunity when you are able to take advantage of these schemes can be time-limited. This can induce a sense of panic amongst those looking to avail themselves of the offers.

Unfortunately those involved in the promotion, operation and installation of these schemes rarely have any understanding of traditional buildings and the harm that can result.

The installation of inappropriate insulation materials may significantly increase the risk of dampness and condensation within the building fabric. Insulation should only be considered after careful analysis of the building fabric has been carried out. To be effective the proposals would need to balance the requirements for protecting building fabric, fire prevention, ventilation and heating strategies. They would also have to incorporate a strategy for carrying out remedial or repair work and future maintenance.

Take care that the installation of ancillary equipment, such as heating systems or microgeneration technology, does not damage the building fabric.

Insulated pipework can take up a lot of space and, when not handled carefully, will result in large holes being formed in the historic structure. The equipment can be large and bulky, and once in place it may prevent access to areas that could require remedial work or maintenance in the future.

Consider the impact that these installations will have on your budget for ongoing maintenance and repair. If you deplete these funds in order to contribute to the finance of these installations, planned maintenance may be put on hold, storing up potential problems in the future.

Fitting modern technology into a traditional building can sometimes be a bit of a squeeze and can block access to elements of the building fabric that require attention in the future...

...Make sure you sort out the fabric before installing the technology.

Trap Number 5

HEAD IN THE SAND

Just as some have an urge to get cracking, others may find the process daunting and try to put as much off as possible.

It is a simple fact frequently overlooked, that all buildings, even modern ones, require regular maintenance. Due in part simply to their age, traditional buildings may have suffered from a lack of maintenance for a prolonged period. The result is an exaggerated impression of decay.

Research shows that most of us tend to be reactive in our approach to building care, dealing with problems as they occur.

Proactive maintenance based on a regular inspection regime will help to identify any potential problems early, before they cause any damage, minimising any repair costs in the future.

Get to know your building, give it a regular check-up, plan repairs and maintenance and keep records. Even when you are not planning major alterations this will be worthwhile. Many public organisations, with a portfolio of traditional buildings, such as the church, have a regular five-year inspection regime for this very reason.

If your building is located adjacent to the street, you may also have a legal duty of care to the public. In recent years, there have been a number of incidents, where members of the public have been badly injured and sometimes killed by masonry falling from traditional buildings.

Above all else, the greatest risk to a traditional building is to leave it empty or vacant. A building that is unused will deteriorate through a lack of repair and maintenance. Defects will go unnoticed and dampness will accumulate within the structure, resulting in the catastrophic failure of roofs and walls. A once valuable asset will become a ruin.

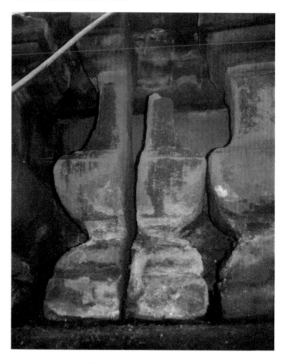

An example of decorative stonework that has become loose and damaged. When inspected, it was found that the stone was not bonded in any way to its surroundings and it was only through good fortune that it had not fallen to the street below.

TUNNEL VISION

A thoughtful approach to not only the space planning but also the ancillary items (light fittings, style of furniture, colour scheme) to create a harmonious space.

It is understandable that the main spaces of the building will be the focus of your attention, but there are details and ancillary spaces and services that will have a major impact on the feel and performance of the spaces and must not be forgotten.

These days even a modest room can be bristling with fixtures and fittings: door ironmongery, light switches, sockets, smoke detectors, alarm sensors, etc. There are a wide range of designs and styles available to ensure that these do not intrude on the visual character of the space.

Finishes not only have a visual impact, but the quality of their surface can impact on the acoustic environment. Hard tiles or finishes like timber floors can create a soundscape that is loud and brash, which might disrupt the feel of the space that you are trying to create. Acoustics are important, whether for clarity of communication in an office space or comfort in a living room.

Ample storage is needed to house the many items that accompany the activities that you have planned for each space.

The current demand for the improved energy performance of buildings has introduced a requirement for larger spaces to accommodate the controls and equipment needed.

Technology is changing and developing with increasing pace and frequency. It is important that services and wiring installations are designed in a manner that enables them to be maintained, upgraded and replaced without major disruption.

Trap Number 7
FALLING OUT WITH THE NEIGHBOURS

Long after any work you are planning is finished, you will continue to have a relationship with your neighbours.

Work on your property may cause significant disturbance to those around you and they may not share your excitement.

Vans and deliveries can block narrow streets and lanes in historic townscapes that were never designed for vehicles. Noise from hammers and power tools can be transmitted through solid structures, causing a great deal of distress to those who are looking for peace and quiet in their own homes.

Do everything you can to avoid working at evenings and weekends.

You will need to take care that any work you do, does not damage or otherwise have an adverse effect on the property of others. Depending on the type of work being planned, you may be well advised to undertake a condition survey of neighbouring properties. This would help to demonstrate, after the work begins, that any problems present in neighbouring properties, were pre-existing and not a result of any work carried out in the course of your project.

If your property is attached to others or part of a larger building, such as a town centre tenement, there may be additional obligations that you must take into consideration. As well as the needs of your own property, there may be a legal requirement to contribute towards the care and maintenance of the larger building in common with the other property owners. You may also have to get their agreement before carrying out any work.

Being considerate to your neighbours can take time. Communicating your intentions, and trying to find a method of delivering the project to minimise disruption for others, may be frustrating. On the other hand, the opportunity to enjoy the fruits of your labour may be significantly diminished if your relationship with the neighbours deteriorates irrevocably.

CHAPTER THREE :

7 TIPS TO BE RECOMMENDED

Well done, you have recognised the challenges and dangers ahead and have resolved to continue in your quest to deliver a successful project. In this chapter I am going to introduce you to useful strategies that will help you on your way.

It is impossible to completely remove risk from the development process, but we can replace unexpected and incalculable risks with those that we can manage and control.

If you adopt a methodical approach and are patient, the process will be more enjoyable, with greater prospects for a successful outcome.

You may recognise a common theme running through the chapter: that of teamwork. Understanding the process and being part of a team is important. Everyone has an important contribution to make, anticipating problems and delivering solutions.

Empty buildings contain many hazards and need to be approached with caution.
Don't enter abandoned buildings on your own.

The first tip in this chapter is **the most important.**

We encourage you to get to know your building in as much detail as possible before carrying out any work, but be careful; survey work is potentially dangerous.

There are many issues relating to safety that cannot be described in detail here. Remember these three points, get professional help and you will start on the right path.

Access

Many parts of your building will be difficult to access.

The use of ladders should be limited to short climbs where the ladder can be placed on stable and level ground. Always get someone to hold the ladder for you and don't overreach where you might lose your balance.

Externally, access can be achieved with the use of a cherry picker, a scaffold or remotely operated drones fitted with an HD camera; however, specialist equipment such as this should only be operated by trained professionals.

Internally, assess the condition of the structure before entering any areas not in everyday use. Timbers may have suffered from decay and may not be able to hold your weight. If you are not sure, do not enter.

DO NOT enter unused spaces or buildings alone.

Always tell someone where you are going and when you are expected to return. Take someone with you. Bring a mobile phone and a torch.

Consider waiting until proper access is provided during the construction stage before carrying out a detailed survey.

Asbestos

Asbestos dust and fibres can be extremely hazardous to your health. Asbestos can be found in a wide range of materials from roof coverings to lino, to toilet cisterns, to pipes and insulation. If you are unsure about any materials that you encounter, do not disturb them; leave the area immediately and contact your architect for advice.

CDM 2015

In the UK, the health and safety of all activities relating to construction works is taken very seriously and is controlled by legislation. This imposes legal duties and responsibilities on all building owners, including private individuals that are planning works to their own homes.

There must be safe methods for carrying out planned works and safe means for maintaining the property in the future. Compliance with these obligations may have an impact on your design ideas, project timetable or proposed methods for carrying out the works.

As a building owner, it is your legal responsibility to ensure that works are planned in a manner that will enable them to be carried out safely. The best way to address these obligations is to appoint a **principal designer** and a **principal contractor** to manage these issues for you.

These roles are specific to the legislation and your **architect** will be able to advise you on the actions required and the associated costs.

Tip Number 2
BUILD YOUR TEAM

The first person you should consider engaging on any project is your architect. Your architect will be able to provide a thorough assessment of your project and identify areas where additional expertise may be required, such as specialist surveys, structural engineering, cost management, etc.

The Principal Designer

In 2015, changes were introduced to the management of safety in relation to any construction work in the UK, including domestic work. You need to be aware that the law requires that clients in the UK appoint a competent **principal designer** to assist in the management of safety for the duration of the project.

Your architect will be able to give you specific advice in relation to your legal duties and many architects are able to provide this as a service to complement their standard service.

Your Architect

The only issue to consider when selecting the professional team for your project should be quality. It is often suggested that quality needs to be balanced with cost, but this is a myth that needs to be debunked.

The cost for professional services is a small percentage of the overall project cost.

Compare the fee charged by someone who is doing the absolute minimum to get you by the various regulations with the fee for an architect who is providing a higher-quality service, looking after your interests, giving advice and anticipating and resolving problems.

You will find that the difference in the fee charged between a minimal service and a quality service is an even smaller fraction of the overall project cost.

This does not mean that more expensive is better; quite often it is not. To avoid the issue of cost interfering in the selection process, first pick your team on their ability and their approach and enquire about the costs only when you have identified the right team.

A quality service provides significant added benefits. The attention to detail that a quality service provides will bring improvements in efficiency, controlling budgets and liaising with the contractor that will achieve cost savings which more than cancel out any additional fee.

Over and above the cost saving, there are additional benefits; a better design, reduced stress and a greater certainty of outcome. Base your decision on quality.

When considering the quality of the architect's service, you need to look at

- Their ability to understand your vision
- Their values
- Their experience and skill

It is important that your architect is committed to building a long-term relationship with you. They will talk you through the development process step by step, discussing your requirements, helping to plan the works and anticipating problems that you might not see.

What do I mean by the architect's values? Well, even when an architect is committed to helping you achieve your goals, each architect will have a unique approach to design and working with their clients. This will be reflected in their work. If the feel of the space is important to you, it is a good idea to work with an architect who delivers a visual style that is similar to the feel that you want to create in your own building.

Ask your architect for images or photographs of previous work and the ideas that underpin their design style. Don't be embarrassed about asking. Architects who are committed to a quality service will appreciate you taking an interest and will welcome the opportunity to discuss their values with you.

Experience and skill can be a matter of examining your architect's qualifications and track record.

In the UK, the use of the title 'architect' is protected by legislation. This legislation recognises that in order to protect clients and their property, it is necessary to provide assurances regarding the quality of the services provided to them. Only those who have successfully undertaken the required training are permitted to describe themselves as architects. Architects are also required to conduct their business to a high standard of professionalism.

Every architect in the UK is listed on the Register of Architects and any member of the public can search the register online to check the credentials of their architect.

There are many businesses offering 'architectural' services. Be careful, this description can lead to misunderstandings. It is a term often used by those who offer technical services but who have not undertaken the extensive training and professional examinations that are required by the law to enable them to call themselves architects.

If in doubt, check the online Register of Architects or ask the service provider for evidence of their membership of ARB. Details for the architects' register are listed on the resources page at the end of the book.

A **conservation architect** is a registered architect who has additional expertise specific to the restoration and renovation of traditional and historic buildings and has undertaken additional training and examination to obtain formal qualifications issued by an accredited organisation.

Funding and regulatory bodies such as Historic Scotland, Historic England, the Heritage Lottery Fund etc. may insist that a conservation architect be included in your team if the building is historically significant or if they are providing financial assistance.

Your Builder

The builder will assemble a team that will be able to offer the range of trades needed to deliver the project.

There are a wide variety of builders but only a limited number with the skills and expertise that are suitable for working with traditional buildings. Those that have the required skills are often true craftsmen and take great care and pride in their work. They have hands-on skill in a specific trade that has been honed over many years.

The builder will manage the site and ensure that each tradesman has the necessary means of access, materials, time and assistance to complete their work. Your builder will work closely with your architect to make sure that the finished building not only performs well but achieves the look and feel that you aspire to.

Your architect will be able to talk with you about potential builders and methods for selecting the most appropriate builder for your project.

Tip Number 3
STAY FOCUSED

Whatever the plans for your property, having a clear set of goals is going to help you make your dream a reality. With clear objectives, it is easier to identify the steps that need to be taken to achieve them.

Setting goals can be as simple as answering a series of questions related to your aspirations for the property.

- What does the property mean to both you and the community?
- How do you want to use the property?
- What is the feel or character of the space that you want to create?

Here are a few pointers to consider when identifying your goals:

- Keep the number of goals as few as possible; limit your list to five clear objectives. The more you have, the more likely it is you will lose focus.
- Try to define your goals as clearly as possible.
- Focus on the type of activity or experience that is important to you, rather than how this is to be achieved. This will help to ensure your goals are both achievable and realistic.

Regularly review your goals. You will find that they will evolve or change over time. It is easy to forget them as your focus moves to more detailed aspects of the project. When you lose sight of these goals, decisions may be taken that conflict with your goals, making them more difficult to achieve.

Tip Number 4
CONTINGENCIES

One of the most important considerations will be to identify how much you can afford to spend on the project and how much your build is going to cost.

When you start adding up costs and establishing a budget, it is easy to assume that everything is going to go exactly as planned. The work will be completed without any changes or adjustments and on time.

The reality is that costs and timescales will change and your plans will need to be flexible to take account of this. Start by being honest from the start, both with yourself and with your architect.

Many critical decisions will be made on the basis of your budget. Make sure that both you and the architect understand what is to be provided within the budget figure:

- Is it the construction cost?
- Is it the construction cost plus professional fees?
- Are furniture, decoration and landscaping included in the budget?
- Is it all of the above, plus local authority fees and charges, taxes?

It is always prudent to include a contingency within your budget to cover unforeseen works that may arise. This is especially important when dealing with older buildings, as there may be any number of surprises lurking behind wall and ceiling finishes.

The amount of contingency required will vary. Where careful and diligent investigation and survey work has been carried out, it is more likely that any potential surprises will have been identified in advance and the contingency may be reduced to reflect this confidence.

Where limited survey work has been carried out, you should provide a more generous contingency. The potential project risks need to be discussed with your architect.

Spliced repair to timber column where the base was rotten; it is not always necessary to replace the whole column...

Tip Number 5
GETTING VALUE FOR MONEY

Obtaining the lowest price for any work that you need done, may seem like a reasonable objective. However this is not as straightforward as you might be led to believe.

When you discuss the project with others, you will be offered all sorts of views and opinions whether these are invited or not. The ability to keep these well-intentioned comments within a meaningful context is essential. No two situations are the same and important aspects of one project may not have been revealed or may not be relevant to your project, making comparison tricky.

Friends or relatives may offer you services for 'mates' rates. These may be well-intentioned and offer the prospect of low costs, but, for all the reasons discussed previously, it is unlikely that you will be able to deliver the project successfully on an informal basis and you may well fall foul of health and safety legislation.

A formal tender with detailed drawings and specification is a common way to obtain prices from a contractor. Its suitability will depend on the extent to which contractors are able to price on the same basis.

This would require each candidate to offer an identical level of service based on exactly the same quantity and quality of work, with a complete understanding of what is required and with no prospect of changes, interruptions or unforeseen surprises.

However hard your team try, there will inevitably be gaps in the information they can provide to contractors. There will be instances where the contractor has to anticipate your requirement. In addition to this, each contractor will have strengths and weaknesses in different areas which may make them more or less suitable for the work in question.

Competitive tendering is therefore not as clear-cut a comparison as is often claimed.

To overcome this drawback, competitive tendering usually needs to be accompanied by an element of quality assessment. Only the contractors that can satisfy criteria balancing quality and cost will be permitted to participate in the tender.

A negotiated tender with selected contractors that have the correct profile of skills and experience for your project is another option to consider.

The success of this approach will rely on the knowledge and expertise of those conducting the negotiation. Your conservation architect will have an important role in helping you to assess the offers submitted to ensure that you receive value for money.

A negotiated approach has the advantage of bringing a contractor with your ideal skill set into the project team early, allowing them to contribute their own expertise to the planning of the construction stage. This will help to reduce risk and increase the opportunity for efficiency and cost saving.

Whichever method you use, selecting a contractor on price alone should not be your objective. The success of your project will depend on a wide range of issues and the quality of the build will have a bearing on future maintenance requirements.

A good job will last longer and reduce your costs in the long term.

Tip Number 6
KEEP CALM AND CARRY ON

Stuff happens, things will inevitably go wrong, but that need not mean that heads should roll.

Building projects require many decisions to be made about the works in advance. As the work progresses, adjustments will be made, information updated, outcomes evaluated and the whole process repeated again and again until the works draw to a close.

With so much information flowing and evolving, errors will occasionally creep in. This is the nature of construction and building contracts have evolved procedures specifically for dealing with these situations. Even so, it is important to promote an atmosphere of trust and openness to ensure that when something inevitably goes wrong, people will be confident about coming forward and be given an opportunity to put things right without fear of humiliation.

Occasionally there will be a financial impact, but this will be offset by the benefits of having a workforce that is working in partnership with you and shares your goals. They will not only be committed to building a high-quality product that will reduce long-term maintenance costs, but by working as a team they will also help to identify efficiencies and savings elsewhere that will balance out the financial bottom line.

The pressure of decision-making and the financial consequences can cause a great deal of stress. Knowing that you have a great team who are working day and night to support you and your objectives will reduce this pressure.

Just as it is important to keep calm, it is also important that you remain consistent, communicate clearly and commit to decisions once they are taken. Tempting as it may be to try and incorporate the latest product that you have only just discovered, try to resist.

Once work has started on site, every change has the potential to disrupt tasks that have been planned weeks in advance, creating inefficiencies and cost overruns. In extreme cases changes may require opening up and re-doing works that have already been completed.

While the rest of the team will try to maintain a professional objectivity, you will be emotionally close to the project. Try to be as clear as possible about what you are looking for. There may be times when you think you have asked for something straightforward, without realising that there are significant consequences.

Work with your architect to make decisions about as many aspects of the work as possible before construction starts. If you are undecided about your preferred colour scheme or visual features and deadlines demand a decision, let your architect guide you.

Tip Number 7
GIVE YOUR BUILDING TIME TO RECOVER

Buildings have their own personalities, especially homes. We form a close relationship with them as we adjust the way we live to the physical space that surrounds us. They offer comfort and security and become the backdrop to so many memories that they become an integral part of the family.

The pattern of light that enters through the windows during the day. The nooks and crannies that become home offices or a child's favourite hideaway. The way the acoustics render our favourite tracks as they filter through from room to room. The fabric heaves and sighs with the changing seasons like a living being. It expands and contracts with temperature changes and settles into a regular routine and pattern of usage that accompanies our lifestyles.

When that pattern suddenly changes, your home can have a panic attack.

This can frequently happen when a home changes ownership, and the new occupants bring new ideas and lifestyles into a house that has functioned well for previous occupants over many years.

Major additions or alterations introduce new loading patterns that unsettle the existing structure and restrict the way the materials previously moved and flexed.

New heating systems can introduce new patterns of expansion and contraction that unsettle the materials and finishes.

Doors and frames can shrink or swell so that they catch or stick. Joints between materials begin to open up causing cracks in paintwork. Pipes can begin to drip.

There are a few things you can do to ensure that any disruption is minimised.

When moving or planning alterations, be sensitive to the architecture and materials, work with the fabric rather than against it. Not only will this help the building, it will reduce your costs.

Be patient and anticipate that the building will require a period of adjustment after any major works.

CHAPTER FOUR :

STAY FLEXIBLE

Now, more familiar with the path that lies ahead, you are in a better position to start thinking about the planning of your project and the various tasks ahead.

There are many ways to approach the challenges and each project will require a unique response. In all cases there will be risks; these can be managed but never eliminated.

The extent of the risk and when this risk materialises will depend on your own particular project strategy.

By way of an example, during the early stages of the project you will be faced with a dilemma:

> Should you incur the cost of undertaking a full investigation of the structure to prepare a fully developed design proposal that you then submit for planning? You will have greater cost certainty that the project is deliverable, but you may not get planning approval in which case the costs incurred may come to nothing.

> Alternatively, do you try to reduce your initial costs by limiting site investigation and submitting a proposal for planning approval early? Once you have planning approval you can then commit to a more detailed investigation knowing that you have permission. However, after the investigation is carried out, you might then find that there is more work required than was initially thought and your project budget is no longer adequate for your proposal.

There is a risk associated with each strategy. Whichever strategy you choose, there is no certainty and risk cannot be avoided.

Eliminating risk entirely is impossible and trying to reduce it to the minimum is frequently counter-productive.

To reduce risk to a minimum, it is necessary to conduct extensive research and planning in advance of any tasks being carried out. You may have a better understanding of the total costs for the works, but it is less likely that the process will identify any significant savings. As a result, you may find that your total expenditure has increased.

This approach will also reduce the flexibility available to the project team to adjust site activities in response to the evolving situation. Opportunities to increase efficiency and reduce costs may be lost.

A flexible approach will accept that there is always going to be risk and uncertainty and will provide a suitable allowance for unforeseen events. If things go well, you will benefit from the saving. Plan for the worst outcome, and hope for the best.

When balancing the scope of works and available budgets it is important to maintain a similarly flexible approach. It is not always necessary to do everything immediately and often the funds aren't available to do this.

You should imagine that you are building a long-term relationship with your building. This should promote a systematic and incremental approach to building improvements.

For example, where gutters are missing and water run-off is damaging the walls, it would be preferable to install plastic uPVC gutter as a temporary measure rather than delay any repair. The plastic gutters can be replaced in the future as part of your longer-term strategy when funds are available.

The development of an incremental plan requires a detailed understanding of the traditional building fabric.

The use of temporary measures must be approached with caution. Installing anything on a temporary basis is an additional cost. Without expert advice, temporary measures could damage the building. They may also contravene local planning controls. A documented strategy for the long-term improvement of the historic fabric would be an essential part of any consultation with the local planning authority.

Work with your architect to identify the goals for your building and develop a step-by-step plan that prioritises actions that will protect and conserve the building fabric.

Experience is the key to understanding advantages and disadvantages of different project strategies and developing a long-term plan that balances competing demands. For example, experience will help with:

- Recognising the limitations on what can be achieved within a given budget.
- Recognising the range and types of risk associated with each decision and the consequences that may arise should a potential risk become a reality.
- Knowing how to manage project expenditure in order to balance project timescales (when certain things are done) with the exposure to potential risks (what could happen if certain things aren't done).

Your architect will be able to talk through the issues that are particular to your project and the alternative options that may be available to you.

CHAPTER FIVE :

WHEN DANGER CALLS

If you have followed the course of this book so far, you will be aware of the importance of getting the right advice, investigating thoroughly, developing a suitable plan of action and, most of all, allowing yourself plenty of time to do things properly. If you are fortunate enough to have time on your side, then I am happy to say that you can skip this chapter...

Unfortunately, there are occasions when good advice just comes too late.

If you suddenly find yourself in a situation where you are responsible for a building in an advanced state of disrepair, then time is not on your side and this is the chapter for you.

A Bit of Sympathy

It is easy to neglect a building by accident. We lead busy lives and often fail to notice small incremental changes in the built environment around us. This is particularly the case with empty buildings.

Isolated buildings sitting in open countryside are often easier to spot, but empty buildings can be found in a multitude of situations. Some building types will have a complex mix of uses which will disguise any deterioration and distract your attention.

A good example would be properties in historic town centres. These are often made up of extended building complexes. Accumulations of traditional buildings that have been extended and joined together over many, many years. As pedestrian routes within the town centres change over time, alleyways and courtyards become closed off and forgotten.

The big mistake is to believe that these buildings are just sitting doing nothing. In fact there is a lot going on, but it is deep down in the heart of the building fabric, hidden from view. You may start to notice the odd slate or roof tile, falling. You may notice some weeds taking seed in the gutters. Perhaps a leaking rainwater pipe staining the wall. If you keep ignoring the outward signs, the deterioration will accelerate until one day the building becomes a concern to the authorities who have a responsibility for public safety.

A Reality Check

When buildings become a hazard to public safety, you have no option but to take action as soon as possible.

You may receive an official notice from the local authority which will identify action that needs to be taken and a deadline for when the works must be completed. Do not underestimate the seriousness of this notice. Should you fail to comply with this notice, the authorities may enter the property, carry out the work themselves and issue you a bill for the work that has been carried out.

When repair work has to be organised and carried out at short notice, you should anticipate paying a premium for all the services, surveys and trades required.

You will need a conservation architect to help you manage the various legal obligations covering safety, building conservation, wildlife and environmental protection. There is little margin for error or delay, so it is important that you assemble a reliable team and you should refer to chapter 3 for further advice.

From the outside, it may look nothing more than a bit untidy to the untrained eye ...

... Inside, the structure is approaching catastrophic failure.

A Five-Step Plan

The first step will be to appoint your **conservation architect.**

Your architect will help you to prioritise the tasks required to make the building safe as soon as possible. They will advise you on the need to appoint other consultants help you to organise the necessary surveys and tradesmen, and help you liaise with the local authority.

The second step is to make the building safe, eliminating any hazards to the public.

This step will need to be organised carefully to ensure that important building features are recorded and protected throughout the work. These emergency measures may be significant, requiring the removal of major structural elements, exposing the building fabric to the weather. Anything with a heritage or architectural value that is removed from the structure should be stored carefully to enable future re-instatement.

The third step will be to install any additional temporary measures necessary to protect the building fabric from the weather.

This step needs to follow the previous one in quick succession, to ensure that any further damage to the building fabric is minimised. Although temporary, the measures need to be designed carefully to ensure that they are durable enough to last until you are ready to carry out a permanent repair.

Interior fittings stripped out and props installed to support the floor and roof above until permanent repairs can be implemented.

The fourth step is to start planning a more permanent repair.

You will need to complete the investigation work and work closely with your conservation architect to consider options for the future restoration and development of the property. It is important that you do not delay this step. The temporary measures installed in the previous step will have only a limited lifespan and need to be replaced while they are still effective.

The fifth step is to carry out the permanent construction works.

The repair work has been carried out, but your work is not over. It is important that you continue to work with your conservation architect to develop a plan for the long-term maintenance, improvement and restoration of the building. Don't make the mistake of delaying this action. If you do not continue to monitor your building it will begin to deteriorate again and you will quickly find yourself back at the start of this chapter.

Conclusion

The moral of this story: if you own a traditional property, it is never too early to call your conservation architect. Even if you believe your property is in good condition, it is worthwhile to give it a regular health check from a professional. Follow the example of bodies with large property portfolios such as the church, the National Trust etc. and obtain a regular five-year inspection.

A conservation architect will be able to spot any potential problems early, when the cost of repair is negligible ensuring the value of your property is maximised.

NEXT STEPS...

I hope you have enjoyed the book and I hope that it has given you a useful insight into the key issues that will contribute to a successful outcome for your project.

With the knowledge you have gained, you will be able to engage in more useful and productive discourse with your architect and project team. When you receive comments or advice that may at first glance appear overly-cautious or non-committal, you may have a better understanding of the reasons behind that.

I have highlighted the common issues that regularly occur on projects based on my own experiences over the years. These are not the only issues that crop up and this book is in no way intended to be an exhaustive or definitive examination of the subject.

I have sought to highlight that the way you approach the project and plan it in advance, is as important as any of the technical activities that are carried out during the building work.

While I haven't discussed the technical aspects of traditional building techniques, I will take this opportunity to highlight one last time: working with traditional buildings and materials requires specific skills and experience. Speak to a **conservation architect** before you start; it will help to avoid costly mistakes later on.

If you are interested in looking at the technical challenges in more detail, you will find some useful resources in the final section of this book.

If you would like to discuss anything contained in the book, offer some feedback or share your own experiences, please feel free to contact me, I would be delighted to hear from you.

Thank you

Calum Maclean . RIAS . RIBA .

c.maclean@aidh.co.uk

USEFUL RESOURCES

Professional Bodies and Organisations

Architects Register
http://www.arb.org.uk

The Architects Registration Board (ARB) is the body responsible in law for managing the list of architects registered to practise in the UK.

The board's website includes details of the standard of service and performance that must be provided by architects.

Royal Institute of British Architects
http://www.architecture.com

The Royal Institute of British Architects champions communities, better buildings and the environment through architecture and its members.

On its website you will find a wealth of information on everything related to architecture and design.

RIAS Directory of Conservation Architects
http://www.rias.org.uk/directory/conservation

The Royal Incorporation of Architects in Scotland (RIAS) provides advice and guidance on all matters related to architecture in Scotland.

The RIAS operates a list of accredited conservation architects.

Conservation Bodies and Organisations

Historic Scotland
http://www.historic-scotland.gov.uk

Historic Scotland provides a wealth of information relating to the technical conservation of historic buildings.

- Undertaking technical and scientific research
- Supporting the perpetuation and understanding of traditional building skills
- Understanding and promoting the use and availability of traditional building materials
- Providing specialist technical and scientific advice
- Providing applied specialist conservation services

Historic England
http://www.historicengland.org.uk/advice/

Historic England is the public body that looks after England's historic environment. It champions historic places, helping people understand, value and care for them.

Institute of Historic Building Conservation
http://www.ihbc.org.uk

The IHBC was established to develop and maintain the highest standards of conservation practice, to support the effective protection and enhancement of the historic environment, and to promote heritage-led regeneration and access to the historic environment for all.

Scottish Lime Centre
http://www.scotlime.org

The Scottish Lime Centre Trust promotes the knowledge and traditional skills required for the conservation, repair and maintenance of the historic built environment.

The trust works nationally and internationally to provide advice and traditional skills training for anyone dealing with a historic structure, be it an A-listed castle or a garden wall.

Society for the Protection of Ancient Buildings
http://www.spab.org.uk

SPAB is involved in all aspects of the survival of buildings which are old and interesting. Its principal concern is the nature of the 'restoration' or 'repair', because misguided work can be extremely destructive.

The Principles of Design and Conservation of Historic Buildings

ICOMOS is a non-governmental international organisation dedicated to the conservation of the world's monuments and sites. The following references provide excellent advice on the philosophy of conservation and the approach that should be taken when dealing with traditional buildings.

THE BURRA CHARTER - ICOMOS

http://australia.icomos.org/wp-content/uploads/The-Burra-Charter-2013-Adopted-31.10.2013.pdf

CHARTER ON THE BUILT VERNACULAR HERITAGE - ICOMOS

http://www.international.icomos.org/charters/vernacular_e.pdf

BS 7913:2013	The only authoritative national UK guide to tackle issues such as ensuring optimum quality of conservation work and appropriate property management and be aimed at everyone, not just the specialists.

Books and References

Buildings of the Scottish Countryside Robert J Naismith (1985), Gollancz	An excellent study of traditional buildings explaining the historic development, design styles and regional variations of historic buildings throughout Scotland.
The Tenement Handbook John Gilbert & Ann Flint (1993), Rutland Press	An illustrated technical manual for traditional Scottish tenements that provides guidance on the management of repairs and maintenance relating to properties that are in multiple ownership.